HOUSEHOLD
TIPS

HOUSEHOLD TIPS

OVER 300 USEFUL AND VALUABLE HOME HINTS

A.L. FOWLER

The advice given in this book dates from
1916 and may contradict current practice.

Front cover: *A tray of dishes to wash* (Mary Evans Picture Library/Joyce Dennys)

First published in 1916
This edition first published in 2011

The History Press
The Mill, Brimscombe Port
Stroud, Gloucestershire, GL5 2QG
www.thehistorypress.co.uk

British Library Cataloguing in Publication Data.
A catalogue record for this book is available from the British Library.

ISBN 978 0 7524 6033 8

Typesetting and origination by The History Press
Printed in the EU for History Press.

To the many efficient and up-to-date housekeepers of our land this book is respectfully dedicated, in the hope that they may find something herein to further increase their efficiency. While the author does not guarantee the reliability of these household helps, they have been carefully compiled from reliable sources and are believed to be efficient if directions are carefully followed.

Contents

CONTENTS

1

THE CARE AND USE
OF GAS APPLIANCES

CARE OF GAS RANGES

In order to get satisfactory and economical service
and a long life, any range or mechanical device must
be kept clean. This applies to the gas range as well, and
we therefore wish to emphasise that the little attention
required is very much worthwhile.

Clean the top, the ovens and removable drip pan
frequently.

Clean broiler griddle and pan every time it is used.

If any burner holes become clogged, clean them
out with a piece of wire or a hairpin.

Keep the air inlets on the shutter at the front of
the burners near the levers clear of dust. The suction at this point draws the dust, which, if allowed to
accumulate, will cause the flame to burn yellow or
red instead of blue.

More ranges rust out than wear out. To keep the range free from rust rub it very frequently with a cloth slightly oiled with any kind of oil or grease, except kerosene or one containing salt; we suggest the use of olive oil or one of its cheaper substitutes. This is done to the best advantage while the range is warm.

When the burners become greasy, remove and wash them thoroughly in soap and hot water. Never black the burners or top grates.

The broiler pan and rack should be kept out of the range when oven is being used or it will rust, warp or chip. It requires the same care any kitchen enamel ware does.

Always leave oven and broiler doors open for a few minutes after lighting the oven burners and after extinguishing them. This will dry the inside of the range and prevent rusting.

USE OF THE RANGE

With reasonable care gas is much cheaper for household cooking than any other fuel.

Every range should be equipped with a top burner lighter which is convenient and economical, as it is just as easy to light a burner as to leave it burning.

Never turn on the gas until you are ready to use it.

Turn off the gas as soon as you are through with it.

Turn down the gas as low as possible to give the required heat. Remember that water boiling rapidly is no hotter than water boiling slowly.

Always open oven door before lighting oven burners.

Plan your cooking so as to use both broiler and oven at once. The same burners heat both. While a roast is in the broiler, bake the cookies, bread, apples or pudding in the oven. When the latter are done, use the oven to cook vegetables or bake biscuits.

To boil foods in the oven, utensils should be set directly on the bottom of the oven.

By following this plan both the time required to cook the meal and your fuel expense will be reduced to a minimum.

BROILING AND ROASTING

Broiling and roasting are the same form of cooking, the former term being applied to thinner and the latter to thicker foodstuffs. They consist of cooking at very high temperatures, obtained only by exposure to the direct flame.

It must be done in the broiler, which should be lighted ten minutes before cooking commences.

Always leave broiler door open and put a little cold water in the bottom of the broiler pan to prevent the food from burning. Place the food to be cooked on the cold rack in the broiling pan.

STEAKS AND CHOPS

Place the meat about two inches from the fire until well seared. Turn over and sear other side in the same way, thus preventing the escape of the juice. Then lower the pan and turn down the gas until the meat is done to taste. For steak allow about ten minutes if one inch thick, fifteen minutes if one and one-half inches thick. For chops allow eight minutes. Cooking may be done faster, but proper tenderness of meats can only be had at the slower rates.

FISH

Place fish on the rack, skin side down, and do not turn. Place rack in lower part of oven. Baste liberally and turn down gas when the fish begins to brown. Allow twenty to thirty minutes.

OTHER FOODS

Chicken, bacon, liver, ham, tripe, and vegetables, such as tomatoes, peppers, Spanish onions, can also be broiled to perfection in a manner similar to above.

ROAST MEATS

Roast meats should be treated the same as steaks and chops, except that after the meat is seared the cooking should be done more slowly, which will, of course, take more time. This part of the cooking can be done with the broiler door closed, or can be done in the upper or baking oven. Allow about twenty minutes to the pound for a roast.

BAKING

Baking is cooking at moderate temperatures in a range oven. The oven should be lighted from five to ten minutes (depending upon the food to be cooked) before the food is put in.

BREAD

Heat the oven about five minutes before using, and bake from forty-five to fifty minutes on the lower rack. Bread should be baked in a hot oven, should continue to rise about fifteen minutes, brown for twenty minutes longer, and bake fifteen minutes longer with a reduced flame.

BISCUITS

Heat oven for ten minutes. Put biscuits in oven and bake for five minutes with full heat, then turn gas off completely and bake five minutes longer.

LOAF CAKE

Heat oven five minutes. Place the cake on the rack about three inches from bottom of oven. Turn gas half on for about thirty minutes when the cake should have fully risen. Increase heat enough to make the top brown and crisp.

LAYER CAKE

Layer cake should be placed in a hotter oven than loaf cake. Heat oven ten minutes. Place cake on rack in centre of oven and turn out the gas for ten minutes. Relight both burners turned half down for twelve or fifteen minutes. If not sufficiently browned increase the heat at the last.

BOILING

Boiling is cooking in water at a temperature of 212 degrees. This is done on the open burners on top of the range. There are three sizes of burners: the giant, the ordinary and the simmerer. In bringing water to boil quickly use the giant burner, then continue boiling on the simmerer or one of the ordinary burners turned low. Do not waste gas by boiling hard. Use covers on kettles.

Green vegetables when boiling retain their colour better if the lid is left off the pot.

STEWING

Stewing is cooking in a small amount of water for a long time at simmering temperature. It is the most economical way of cooking the cheaper cuts of meat. The simmering burner should be used for this cooking.

TOASTERS

Bread toasters placed on the top burners of a gas range supply a quick and the most satisfactory method of preparing toast. Large quantities of toast can be made to advantage in the broiler.

GAS WATER HEATERS

Gas water heaters supply the most economical and convenient source of hot water obtainable.

The automatic water heaters are made to heat water instantly and automatically upon opening any hot water tap in the system. These heaters are made in various capacities from two to eight gallons per minute.

Circulating tank heaters which are attached to the kitchen boiler have to be lighted every time they are used.

Usually the heater is lighted a few minutes before hot water is required, the time depending upon the amount likely to be used. A thirty gallon tank may be heated in approximately one hour. Sufficient hot water for an average bath may be had in fifteen minutes. The most economical way to handle the circulating tank heater, when water is needed for a bath, is as follows: light heater and turn on tap so that the water will flow into the tub as quickly as it is heated in the tank. This is usually at the rate of one gallon per minute.

According to the city ordinance, in residences where water meter check valves are installed on the water service, the consumer should supply a safety water relief valve before connecting any hot water system. This must be done to take care of the expansion.

GAS FLAT IRONS

The gas flat iron is a most satisfactory and economical household appliance.

FURNACE CONNECTIONS

A pipe coil should be placed in every furnace and connected to the hot water tank in order to insure an economical supply of hot water during the period when the furnace is in use. This makes it possible to use the gas range in the kitchen and enjoy its convenience and economy the year round.

ALL-GAS KITCHENS

All-gas kitchens embodying the foregoing appliances are in general use owing to their convenience and economy.

Details regarding these kitchen appliances and other gas appliances, such as fireplace kindlers, furnace kindlers, coke box kindlers, rubbish burners, gas steam radiators, gas water radiators, safety garage heaters and ironing machines may be obtained from your Gas Company. Telephone them, for their salesmen are always glad to serve you.

DEMONSTRATOR

Most gas companies have a practical and expert demonstrator whose services are free. When any gas appliance is not giving perfect satisfaction in every way, or once a year on general principles, you should ask the demonstrator to call.

GAS LIGHTING

Correct, healthful and pleasing lighting conditions do more than anything else to brighten, modernise and make comfortable the house of today. Poor light is poor economy in more than one sense of the term.

'Poor light' may mean too little or too much light, a wrong kind of light or a misplaced source of light. Any of these conditions cause eye strain. Eye strain results in eye troubles and inevitably affects the general health. Furthermore, the well lighted home is an attractive centre for the family, while a badly lighted house creates gloom and a restless atmosphere.

Gas light offers convenience in lighting and beauty in its fixtures.

Gas light presents the real economy of the best at the least cost.

All new houses should be piped for gas. Even an old house can be equipped with ceiling, wall and base-board outlets with but little expense or inconvenience to you. Your Gas Company will also help you to select just the fixtures and burners you need to harmonise with the decorations in your home and to supply the best possible light for each room.

At your call, the Company will keep your equipment in thoroughly efficient condition. You should use only the best gas mantles. It sells them at cost to you in order to encourage their use – cheap mantles are cheap in first cost and expensive in the long run.

Your Gas Company prides itself on being 'at your service.'

2

ELECTRICAL APPLIANCES

ELECTRIC SERVICE IN THE HOME

The home that is completely wired has at hand a tireless electric servant-of-all-work; for the past few years have seen the invention and perfection of devices for doing household labour of practically every description. These are of practical economy not only when used by the housewife, but also in making domestic help more efficient and better satisfied.

In addition to the almost universal use of electricity for lighting, with every facility for flexibility and convenience in connecting and control, electricity may be absolutely depended upon today for washing, wringing, drying and ironing the clothes, for sweeping and dusting, for polishing, for cleaning silver and brightwork, for all cooking, for such culinary processes as beating eggs, mixing bread, grinding meat or coffee, turning the ice cream freezer or sharpening knives, or, on emergency, for heating or cooling the house. And (contrary to popular belief), in most of these cases electricity offers an opportunity for actual domestic economy.

Electricity is no longer a rich man's luxury, for its convenience, cleanliness, time saving and economy, as shown by the following pages, have made it every man's necessity.

ALL-ELECTRIC HOMES

The model home is electrically lighted, has the kitchen equipped with an electric range, electric dish-washer, electric kitchen set for beating eggs, grinding, mixing and polishing; the dining-room equipped with electric coffee percolator, electric samovar and an electric toaster; laundry equipped with electric washing machine, motor-driven mangle heated by gas or electricity, and an electric iron. A vacuum cleaner is essential in every household. Other appliances which will prove their value if once tried are heating pads, vibrators, heating or disk stoves, luminous radiators, sewing machines, fans, pressing iron for the sewing-room and Christmas tree outfits.

ELECTRIC RANGE

Cooking by electricity is an ideal method, and the electric range makes it practical. Every housewife should be familiar with its advantages as it provides the most satisfactory results.

The electric range is reliable, efficient and durable. It saves time, work, worry and watching. It promotes safety, comfort and cleanliness.

The electric range is convenient and easy to operate, as the heat is always instantly available and readily regulated at the turn of a switch. Cooking becomes a certainty, as the same switch position always provides the same amount of heat. All the heat is concentrated on the cooking and there is no excess heat wasted on other parts of the range or radiated out into the room. Ordinary cooking utensils are used as with other ranges.

Cooking with an electric range can be done at a reasonable cost in consideration of the many inherent advantages above referred to.

The roasting of meat to the exact degree desired need not be the dread of the cook when an electric oven is available. The uniformity and reliability of the heat of the electric oven facilitates the roasting of meat without constant attention and worry.

Electric broiling insures tender chops and steaks, as the surface of the meat is quickly seared and all its juicy tenderness is retained.

In order to facilitate the use of the electric range, your Lighting Company gives an instruction book with every installation.

ELECTRIC DISHWASHER

After each meal scrape off the dishes and place them in the washer in such a position that the water can be thrown against both sides of them. It is convenient to accumulate enough dishes to fill the washer, as it may thereby become possible to do all of the day's dishes in one washing.

Shake washing powder or liquid soap into the machine and add one-quarter of a cup of ammonia. Pour in the right amount of hot water from tap (according to instructions with machine) and allow the machine to run about ten minutes. Then let the water run out and pour in a little more to wash out the sediment. Close the drain and pour in boiling water which acts as a rinsing water. Run the machine two minutes more and drain. Raise cover immediately after the machine is stopped to let the steam out. The dishes will dry by themselves with high polish, but it is necessary to wipe the silver and glassware.

The washer is then ready to be used as a storage for dishes until needed again.

VACUUM CLEANER

There are many good electric vacuum cleaners on the market, all of which operate on the same general principle of suction. The Hoover, however, has a motor-driven brush in addition, which acts as a sweeper.

Oil the motor with a drop or two each time it is used, according to the directions given with the machine. If using a Hoover, the brush bearings should not be oiled as they are made of wood.

Should the brush become stuck it is due to threads, string and hair which have been collected by it. Remove the brush according to directions supplied with the machine and free all the bearings.

Clean the bag after using by carefully removing it from the machine and shaking the dirt on a newspaper.

Once a month the machine should be cleaned by taking off the bag, lifting the machine from the carpet and allowing the machine to run for a couple of minutes.

SEWING MACHINE

Follow directions supplied with the machine as to oiling and proper size of needle, thread, etc. Do not make any adjustments unless you are sure you know how. These adjustments require patience, as the adjusting screws must be turned a very little at a time to note the effect produced. Do not run the machine at too high a speed as this will shorten its life.

When putting a motor on a foot-power machine be sure that the old machine is not over-speeded.

If your machine is provided with a foot release be sure that the release entirely cuts off current, otherwise the motor will run very hot.

FLAT IRON

There are several makes of electric irons which do excellent work and have a long life. The standard sizes are three, six and eight pounds. The six-pound iron is best adapted for general household use.

If the iron becomes too hot, disconnect the lead from the iron. In case the terminals become corroded, rub them with a piece of fine emery cloth to remove corrosion. If the contacts become corroded or bent they should be replaced.

Your Lighting Company maintains a repair department for all heating and cooking appliances. Telephone Sales Department.

ELECTRIC LAMPS

Mazda lamps are the most efficient lamps obtainable and their use is recommended for all classes of service.

Your electric bills depend upon the watts per lamp and the number of hours of use. Please note that the Mazda lamps give on the average two and one-half times as much light for the same cost as the Gem carbon lamps.

RESIDENTIAL LIGHTING

In most cases the following recommendations of Mazda lamp sizes will be found most satisfactory in the home. Frosted lamps are recommended wherever the direct rays of the lamp may strike the eye, as the frosting diffuses the light.

PARLOUR

1. Bracket chandelier	1–60 watt
2. Bracket chandelier	2–40 watt
3. Bracket chandelier	3–25 watt
Side wall fixtures for decorative purposes	10 watt, all frosted
Side wall fixtures for good general illumination	25 or 40 watt, all frosted

HALL

Small hall   1–10 watt
Large hall   1–25 watt

PORCH

Ceiling light   1–10 watt
Side bracket   1–25 watt
If used for reading light   1–60 watt

BEDROOM

Ceiling light   1–40 watt
Side bracket   1–40 watt or 2–25 watt

SITTING-ROOM

Same as parlour. A well shaded reading lamp with a
40 or 60 watt all-frosted bulb.

DINING-ROOM

Dome   1–60 watt
                                 bowl frosted

Two or three light shower	25 watt bowl frosted
Semi-indirect	1–60 or 100 watt clear

BATHROOM

Ceiling or side brackets	25 watt

KITCHEN

Ceiling light	1–40 or 60 watt bowl frosted
Side bracket over sink	1–25 watt bowl frosted

ATTIC

25 watt

CELLAR

In installing lamps for the cellar the time they are lighted should be borne in mind. As this is short, the expense of running larger lamps – 25 watt and 40 watt – is insignificant. The following locations should be provided for:

Bottom of cellar stairs	25 watt
Work bench	40 watt
Laundry	40 watt
Vegetable and fruit cellar	25 watt
Lamp in front of furnace	60 watt

This latter lamp is usually close enough to also illuminate the coal bin.

CARE OF LAMPS AND FIXTURES

Lamps and fixtures should he cleaned once a month to insure the maximum efficiency. Reliable tests have shown that dirty glassware reduces effective illumination from ten to fifty per cent.

FIXTURE RECOMMENDATIONS FOR THE HOUSE

Parlour

| Ceiling fixtures | Indirect or semi-indirect |
| Side fixtures | Semi-indirect |

Baseboard receptacles for table or floor lamps.

Hall
One ceiling fixture equipped with two lamps wired so that one or both lamps may be operated as desired. This arrangement provides for a night light.

Sitting-room and Library
Same as parlour.

Bedroom
One ceiling semi–indirect fixture.
Side brackets near dressing table, or,
Rigid pendant for use over centre of dressing table.
Baseboard outlet near bed for heating pad or reading lamp.

Dining-room
Indirect or semi–indirect fixture.
Baseboard or floor outlet for toaster and percolator.
Floor call button attached to kitchen buzzer.

Bathroom
One side bracket on each side of mirror.
    One side wall receptacle for curling iron, shaving mug and luminous radiator.

Kitchen
One centre ceiling light, one side bracket over sink and one side wall outlet for iron and washing machine.

Cellar

Five outlets should be provided for proper illumination, one at foot of stairs, one at work bench, one in fruit and vegetable cellar and one in front of furnace located so as also to illuminate the coal bin.

A control switch and telltale lamp should be provided in the kitchen.

Attic

Two outlets are usually sufficient. A control switch and telltale lamp should be provided in the hall.

Clothes Press

A rigid pendant with a chain-pull socket should be provided for each dark clothes press.

It is most convenient and practical to have these lights operated by an automatic switch which is opened and closed by the closing and opening of the closet door. This provides a light immediately the door is opened, while when the door is shut one may be sure that the light has not been left burning.

GENERAL

Baseboard outlets should be installed in all rooms for the use of vacuum cleaner, fans, or other portable appliances.

Bell-ringing transformers which provide current for door bells and buzzers should be installed for each apartment.

Emergency gas lights should be provided for the halls, kitchen, dining-room and bathroom.

If any special requirements are not provided for in the above recommendations your Lighting Company will be glad to give you expert advice free of charge. They pride themselves on being at your service.

WIRING HINTS

The service entrance should be of sufficient capacity to care for additional load in the form of electric heating, cooking and other domestic appliances. The branch circuits should be heavy and numerous enough to care for additional outlets for lighting and appliances as found desirable. Your Lighting Company will be glad to go over your plans with you.

The electric meters should be located in the cellar near the gas meter, as this will save you the annoyance of metre readers and testers going through the house to the attic.

Be sure and install control switches and telltale lamps on cellar and attic lights.

Provide three-way switches in the halls so that the hall lights may be controlled from either the first or second floor.

All ceiling outlet lighting, and wherever desirable, side bracket lighting, should be controlled by wall switches. These switches should preferably be of the push-button type rather than of the snap-switch type. In general the best location for these switches is on the wall of the room right next to the door which is the entrance most frequently used.

FUSES

Fuses on your electrical wiring act in the same capacity as a safety valve on a steam boiler. Whenever there is an overload on the circuit or a short circuit these fuses blow and relieve the strain on your wiring.

When in doubt or when in need of suggestions, 'phone the Sales Department of your Lighting Company.

3

IN THE KITCHEN

Use Sand Soap to Sharpen the Food Chopper – If the knives of your food chopper become black and dull, run a piece of sand soap, or scouring brick, through the chopper as you would a potato. It will brighten and sharpen the knives and they will cut like new. Use pulverised sand soap or the scouring brick with which you scour.

Kerosene for Water Bugs – A small quantity of kerosene poured down the drain pipe occasionally will stop annoyance from this pest.

To Prevent a Glass from Breaking when pouring hot water in it, first put a spoon in the glass. This method can also be used when pouring hot soup or any hot liquid in any fragile receptacle.

When Butter is Too Hard to spread easily, turn a heated bowl upside down over the butter dish for a few minutes. This will thoroughly soften the butter without melting it.

To Open Fruit Jars – Strips of emery board, about one inch wide and eight inches or so long, will be found useful to loosen obstinate fruit jar tops. Just place the strip around the edge of the top, and give it a twist.

To Keep Refrigerator Sweet – A lump of charcoal should be placed in the refrigerator to keep it sweet. When putting your best tea or coffee urn away, drop a small piece of charcoal in it and prop the lid open with a toothpick.

Currycomb for Scaling Fish – A currycomb is better than a knife for scaling fish, as it protects the hands.

Cornpopper for Toasting Bread – The cornpopper can be used for toasting odds and ends of stale bread which would otherwise be wasted.

To Prevent Stains Under the Nails – Dip the ends of the fingers in melted tallow before beginning a task which is likely to stain them.

To Remove Stains from the Hands, rub them with a piece of lemon.

Starch to Prevent Chapped Hands – Use starch which is ground fine to prevent chapped hands. Every time the hands are washed and rinsed thoroughly, wipe them off, and, while they are yet damp, rub a pinch of starch over their entire surface. Chapping is then not likely to occur.

Wisp Brush for Greasy Pans and Kettles – A small wisp brush is better for cleaning greasy pans and kettles than the string mop you use for the dishes. A little soap powder sprinkled on them makes a fine suds for the tinware and cooking utensils.

Best Way to Strain Soup – When straining soup set a coarse strainer inside of a fine one and pour the liquid through both; you will thus avoid clogging the fine one with pieces of meat and broken bones.

How to Crack Pecan Nuts – Almost all housewives know how very hard it is to crack pecan nuts and get the meats out whole. Pour boiling water over the nuts and let them stand tightly covered for five or six hours. The nut meats may then be extracted easily without a trace of the bitter lining of the nut. Use a nut cracker and crack lightly all around the nuts. The work is quickly done and is not at all like the tedious process of picking out the meats from the dry nuts. The meats nearly always come out whole.

Lemon Squeezer for Making Beef Juice – When one has to make beef juice in small quantities which does not warrant buying an expensive meat-press, use instead a lemon squeezer. This can be sterilised by boiling and kept absolutely clean. One can press out several ounces in a very few minutes.

Quick Way to Peel Carrots – Use a coarse grater to peel carrots. A few passes over the grater will rid the carrots of their skins quicker than any other method.

Proper Way to Slice Bacon – To slice bacon properly, always place it rind down, and do not attempt to cut through the rind until you have the desired number of slices. Then slip the knife under them and cut them free of the rind, keeping as close to it as possible.

When Cream is on the Turn – When the sweetness of the cream is doubtful and there is no more on hand and it must be used, a pinch of soda will keep it from curdling, even in hot coffee.

To Prevent Musty Teapot – When putting away a silver teapot, or one that is not in everyday use, place a little stick across the top underneath the cover. This will allow fresh air to get in and prevent mustiness.

Lemon or Orange Peel for Tea Caddy – Thoroughly dry the peel from an orange or a lemon, and place it in the tea caddy. This will greatly improve the flavour of the tea.

Heat Lemons Before Squeezing – In using lemons, heat them thoroughly before squeezing and you will obtain nearly double the quantity of juice that you would if they had not been heated.

To Keep Teakettle from Rusting – A clean oyster shell placed in the teakettle will keep out rust.

To Clean Gas Stove Burners – Pick the holes open with a large pin and apply a vacuum cleaner to take out the particles of dirt.

Flour for Burning Kerosene – Wheaten flour is the best extinguisher to throw over a fire caused by the spilling and ignition of kerosene. This should be a matter of common knowledge, since flour is always within convenient reach.

Use for Old Newspapers – Old newspapers clean stoves beautifully, as well as being useful for polishing kitchen windows.

To Take Rust from Flat-Irons, tie some yellow beeswax or paraffin in a cloth, and when the iron is warm, but not hot enough to use, rub with the wax and then rub it through sand or salt.

A Good Stove Polisher – A piece of burlap is a very good polisher for the kitchen stove or range when it is hot. It does not burn readily, and for that reason is better than flannel or cotton cloth or paper.

Wire Rack for Use Under Pies – When taking pies from the oven, do not put them on the flat surface of the table to cool unless a high wire rack is put under them. The rack helps to keep the crust crisp and they will not be soggy.

Marble Slab or Plate Glass for Mixing Board – For mixing cake and pastry an old marble slab or a piece of plate glass is better than a wooden board.

To Prevent Cakes from Burning – Sprinkle the bottom of the oven with fine, dry salt to prevent cakes, pies, and other pastry from burning on the bottom.

Wooden Bowl When Washing Silver – When washing silver, use a wooden tub or bowl if possible. There will be less danger of the silver getting scratched or otherwise damaged.

Tissue Paper for Greasy Dishes – Very greasy dishes should be wiped with soft tissue paper before being washed.

To Skin Tomatoes Easily – Tomatoes nearly always have to be skinned before being used. To do this easily, place them in a basin and pour boiling water over them. Let stand a minute, and then drain. Another method is to rub the tomatoes all over with the back of a knife to loosen the skins before peeling. This is said to be better than scalding.

To Peel Sweet Potatoes Easily – Before putting sweet potatoes in the oven, grease the skins and they can then be peeled easily and without any waste of the potato.

To Prevent Roasted Meat from Drying Out – To prevent roasted meat, which is to be served cold, from drying out and losing its flavour, wrap it in cheesecloth while it is still hot.

When Food is Too Salty – When you have put too much salt into cooking food, stretch a clean cloth tightly over the kettle and sprinkle a table-spoonful of flour over the cloth. Then allow the contents of the kettle to steam and in a few moments the flour will absorb the surplus salt.

To Remove Fish Odour from Hands – A few drops of ammonia in the water in which you wash your hands will remove all fishy odour from the hands after preparing fish for cooking.

To Remove Onion Smell from Pans – The disagreeable smell of onions which clings to pots and pans so stubbornly can be quickly removed by washing and drying the pans, then scouring them with common salt, and placing them on the stove until the salt is brown. Shake often, then wash the pans as usual.

To Prevent Onions from Making the Eyes Water – Scalding water poured over onions will keep the eyes from watering.

Hint When Baking Bread – When baking bread or rolls, put a saucepan full of boiling water into the oven. The steam rising from it will keep the crust smooth and tender.

To Make Meat Tender – A tablespoonful of vinegar added to tough meat while it is boiling or roasting will make it more tender.

To Keep the Lid on a Boiling Pot – A teaspoonful of butter dropped into the water in which you are boiling dry beans, or other starchy vegetables, will stop the annoyance of having the lid of the pot jump off, as it will otherwise do. The butter acts the same as oil on troubled waters and keeps it calm and manageable.

To Take Fish Taste from Forks and Spoons – To remove the taste and smell of fish from forks and spoons, rub them with a small piece of butter before washing. All taste and smell will thus be entirely removed.

How to Judge Mushrooms – Sprinkle a little salt on the gills of mushrooms to judge their fitness to eat. If the gills turn black the mushrooms are fit for food; if they turn yellow, the mushrooms are poisonous.

Orange Peel for Cake Flavouring – Do not throw away orange peel, but dry in the oven. Grate the yellow part and use for flavouring cakes. It will give a delicious orange taste.

How to Prevent Fish from Breaking Up When Frying – When frying fish, if the pieces are put in the hot fat with the skin side uppermost, and allowed to brown well before turning, there will be no possibility of the fish breaking up.

To Remove Cake from Tin – When taking a cake from the oven, place the cake tin on a damp cloth for a moment and the cake will turn out of the tin quite easily.

Lemon Juice for Boiling Rice – A few drops of lemon juice added to boiling rice will help to keep the grains separate and will make them white.

Onion for Baked Beans – Bake a small onion with your baked beans to prevent indigestion and add to their fine flavour.

Hint for Baking Gems – When filling gem pans with batter leave one pan without batter and fill with water. This will prevent the gems from burning on top.

Sandpaper for Cleaning Pots – Always keep a piece of fine sandpaper by the sink with which to clean pots.

To Prevent Cake from Sticking to Tins after baking, first grease the tins and then dust them with flour. Lightly beat out the loose flour, leaving only that which sticks to the grease. This does away with the old-fashioned method of lining the pans with greased paper.

To Peel Apples Easily – Pour boiling water over the cooking apples and they will be much easier to peel.

This will be found a considerable saving of time when busy.

When Bread is Too Brown – When bread is baked in too hot an oven and the outside crust gets too brown, do not attempt to cut it off, but as soon as the bread gets cold rub it over with a coarse tin grater and remove all the dark-brown crust.

Mustard for Removing Odours from the Hands – Ground mustard is excellent for cleaning the hands after handling onions and other things with disagreeable odours.

Economy in Use of Candles – A candle which has burned too low to remain in the candlestick can be used to the very end if removed from the stick and placed on a penny or other small, flat piece of metal.

To Get Rid of Spiders – A good way to rid the house of spiders is to take pieces of cotton wool, saturate them with oil of pennyroyal and place them in their haunts.

To Rid the Kitchen of Flies – Take a cup of vinegar and place it on the stove where it will simmer enough to make an odour.

To Clear Beetles Out of Cupboards and larders, sprinkle a little benzine over the boards. This method will kill the eggs as well as the insects.

To Drive Cockroaches Away – Powdered gum camphor will drive cockroaches away if sprinkled about their haunts.

To Remove Egg Stains from Silver – Egg stains can be removed from silver by rubbing it with table salt on a wet rag.

To Polish Taps – Nothing is better for scouring a tap than the half of a lemon after the juice has been squeezed out. After scouring, wash it and it will shine like new. An orange peel will also give good results.

For Scorched Vegetables or Other Food – When vegetables or other foods become scorched, remove the kettle at once from the stove and put it into a pan of cold water. In a quarter of an hour the suggestion of scorch will be nearly if not entirely gone.

When Cake is Scorched – If a cake is scorched on the top or bottom, grate over it lightly with a nutmeg-grater instead of scraping it with a knife. This leaves a smooth surface for frosting.

To Make Muffins and Gems Lighter – Muffins and gems will be lighter if, after greasing your pans you place them in the oven a few moments and let them get hot before putting in the batter.

To Make Pie Crust Flaky – To make pie crust flaky, try adding half a spoonful of vinegar to the cold water when mixing.

To Make Apple Pie Tender – If you are in doubt whether the apples in your open-top pies are cooking tender, just invert another pie pan over the pie and the steam will serve to cook the apples thoroughly.

To Make Fowl Tender – After a turkey or chicken is cleaned, the inside and outside should be rubbed thoroughly with a lemon before the dressing is put in. It will make the meat white, juicy and tender.

To Prevent Meat from Scorching – When roasting meat, and there is danger that it will become too brown, place a dish of water in the oven. The steam arising from it will prevent scorching and the meat will cook better. A piece of greased paper placed over the meat is also considered good.

To Keep Eggs from Popping When Cooking – Mix a tablespoonful of flour in the hot grease in which eggs are to be cooked, and break the eggs into this. You will also find that the flour gives the eggs a better flavour.

To Remove Egg Shells When Cooking – If a piece of shell gets into the egg when breaking eggs into a bowl, just touch it with a half shell and it can easily be removed.

To Keep Yolks of Eggs Fresh – Yolks of eggs which are not wanted for immediate use can be kept good for several days by dropping them into cold water and keeping in a cool place – the cooler the better.

To Prevent Boiling Eggs from Cracking – The four following suggestions are given in regard to boiling eggs. Use the one best suited to the purpose:

When Boiling Eggs, wet the shells thoroughly in cold water and they will not crack.

To Prevent Eggs from Bursting While Boiling, prick one end of each of the eggs with a needle before placing them in the water. This makes an outlet for the air and keeps the shells from cracking.

If Eggs Which You Are About to Boil Are Cracked, add a little vinegar to the water and they can then be boiled as satisfactorily as undamaged ones.

A Spoonful of Salt should be added to the water in which slightly cracked eggs are boiled. The salt will prevent the white of the egg from coming out.

Worn-Out Broom for Floor Polisher – When a long-handled broom becomes worn out, instead of throwing it away, tie a piece of felt or flannel cloth around the head and make a good floor polisher. It will make work much easier and also keep linoleum in good condition. Footmarks can be rubbed off at any time without stooping.

To Clean a Slender Flower Vase fasten a piece of an old sponge onto a stick and push it down into the vase; this will also be found useful for cleaning decanters and water bottles.

To Keep Bread Fresh – Wash a potato, wipe it dry and put it in your breadpan. It will keep the bread fresh for several days.

To Freshen Old Lemons – Lemons that have become old and dry can be made fresh and juicy again by putting them in a pan of hot water and keeping the water at an even temperature for about two hours.

A More Effective Dishcloth for Cleaning – In knitting dishcloths it is a good plan to put in several rows of hard-twisted cord. This hard part of the cloth will clean many surfaces on which it is not advisable to use scouring soap or metal.

To Clean Linoleum, use skimmed milk instead of water. It will keep it glossy, and will not rot it as water does.

A Good Remedy for Burns – Cover a soft cloth with a thick layer of scraped raw potato (Irish) and apply it to the burned part. The potato should be renewed as often as necessary to keep it moist.

For Burns and Light Scalds – At once coat the burned or scalded spot with mucilage and the smarting will cease almost instantly. If the burn is quite deep, keep it covered with a paste made of cold water and flour; do not allow the paste to get dry until the smarting stops.

A Good Way to Save Gas – Read the pages in the front of this book.

Brush for Removing Silk from Corn – When preparing corn on the ear for the table, or for canning purposes, use a small hand brush to remove the silk. It will do the job more thoroughly and quicker than it can be done with the fingers.

To Remove Grease Spots from the Kitchen Floor – Apply alcohol to the spots and you will be surprised to find how easily they can be removed. The small amount of alcohol necessary to be used need not soil the hands.

To Open a Jar of Fruit or Vegetables Which Has Stuck Fast – Place the jar in a deep saucepan half full of cold water; bring it to a boil and let it boil for a few moments. The jar can then be opened easily.

To Identify Dishes Which Have Been Loaned – When taking dishes or silver to a picnic or other public gathering, place a small piece of surgeon's plaster on the bottom of each dish and on the under side of the handles of spoons and forks. On this plaster mark your initials (in indelible ink if possible). The plaster will not come off during ordinary washing, but can later be removed by putting it in a warm place until the adhesive gum melts.

Tablet or Slate for Kitchen Memoranda – Keep in the kitchen a tablet with a pencil tied to it, or a ten-pence slate and pencil hung upon the wall. The day's work is easier and smoother if you plan each morning the special tasks of the day and jot them down, checking them off as accomplished. Planning the day's meals in advance results in better balanced menus. Writing down all groceries and household supplies as needed will save time when you go to the store or the order boy calls.

To Fasten Food Chopper Securely – Before fastening the food chopper to the table, put a piece of sand-paper, large enough to go under both clamps, rough side up, on the table; then screw the chopper clamps up tight and you will not be bothered with them working loose.

To Remove Insects from Vegetables which are being washed, put a pinch of borax in the water. It will bring any live insect to the surface at once.

To Clean Rust and Stains from Tin – Tins that have become rusty or stained may be cleaned by rubbing well with the cut surface of a raw potato which has been dipped in a fine cleaning powder.

To Polish Glass – After washing glass, polish with dry salt.

Lemon Juice for Cut Glass – Lemon juice is fine for polishing cut-glass tumblers. These pretties are so delicate there is always danger of breaking the stems. Fill a pan half-full of cold water, place a cloth in the bottom and then add the juice of an entire lemon. Just dipping a tumbler about in this cleans and polishes it and it only needs drying with soft linen.

Many Uses of Ammonia – As a time saver it is unequalled when washing woodwork and windows. It is fine for cleaning carpets on the floor. They should be swept well and the broom washed; then brush again with water. They will look much brighter, and if there is a lurking moth in the carpet this treatment will destroy it. Ammonia will set colour, remove stains and grease, and soften fabrics.

A light soap suds with a few drops of ammonia added will give a sparkle to ordinary pressed glass and china impossible to secure without it.

Hints for Oil Lamps and Chimneys – The five following paragraphs contain some good suggestions for the use of oil lamps:

Put a Small Lump of Camphor Gum in the body of an oil lamp and it will greatly improve the light and make the flame clearer and brighter. A few drops of vinegar occasionally is said to give the same results.

To Prevent Lamp Chimney from Cracking – A common hairpin placed astride the top edge of a lamp chimney will keep it from cracking from the heat, and will greatly prolong its life.

Gas and Lamp Chimneys, earthenware and baking dishes can be toughened before using by putting them into cold water which is heated gradually until it boils and then cooled slowly.

When Washing Your Lamp Chimneys, lift them out of the water and set them on the hot stove; they will not break. Let them steam; then wipe on a clean cloth and they will be as clear as crystal.

Take Your Lamp Wicks When New and soak them thoroughly in good apple vinegar and you will be delighted with the result. Do not wring them out, but hang them near a stove or lay out on a plate until dry. This treatment will double the lighting power of your lamps or lanterns. With wicks prepared in this way, only one cleaning each week is necessary, as the wicks will not smoke and the chimney and globe will not blacken around the top.

To Mend Broken China, Etc. – The four following methods of mending china, etc., are all considered good:

To Mend Broken China – Mix well a teaspoonful of alum and a tablespoonful of water and place it in a hot oven until quite transparent. Wash the broken pieces in hot water, dry them, and while still warm coat the broken edges thickly; then press together very quickly, for it sticks instantly.

To Mend Broken Crockery – White lead is one of the few cements that will resist both heat and water. Apply it thinly to the edges of the broken pieces, press them tightly together and set aside to dry.

A Cheap Cement for Broken China is lime mixed with the white of an egg. Take only sufficient white of an egg to mend one article at a time, and mix thoroughly with a small quantity of lime.

To Mend China successfully melt a small quantity of pulverised alum in an old spoon over the fire. Before it hardens rub the alum over the pieces to be united, press them together and set aside to dry. After drying they will not come apart, even when washed with hot water.

Embroidery Hoops and Cheesecloth for Cooling Dishes – When putting puddings or other dishes out of doors to cool, use a cover made of embroidery hoops of proper size with cheesecloth put in as a piece of embroidery is. The contents will be safe from dust and at the same time the air can circulate freely. The hoops will keep the cloth from getting into the contents and also weigh just enough to keep it from blowing off.

To Clean Mica in Stove Doors – To clean the mica in stove doors, rub it with a soft cloth dipped in equal parts of vinegar and cold water.

To Clean Tarnished Silver, use a piece of raw potato dipped in baking soda.

For Tarnished Silverware – If the silverware has become badly tarnished, put it in an aluminium dish, cover it with water, and boil it up for a short time. It will come out bright and clean.

To Clean White Knife Handles – To clean and whiten ivory-handled knives which have become yellow with age, rub with fine emery paper or sandpaper.

To Prevent Rust in Tinware – If new tinware is rubbed over with fresh lard and thoroughly heated in the oven before being used, it will never rust afterward, no matter how much it is put in water.

To Remove Rust from Tinware – To remove rust from tinware, rub the rusted part well with a green tomato cut in half. Let this remain on the tin for a few minutes; then wash the article and the rust will have vanished.

Kerosene for Tinware Stains, Etc. – Kerosene removes stains from tinware, porcelain tubs and varnished furniture. Rub with a woollen cloth saturated with it; the odour quickly evaporates.

To Preserve Enamel Pans – If new enamel pans are placed in a pan of water and allowed to come to a boil and then cooled, they will be found to last much longer without burning or cracking.

To Prevent Dust When Sweeping – Wet the broom before starting to sweep; it makes it more pliable and less hard on the carpet's pile and also prevents dust from arising.

To Clean Paint or Rust from Linoleum – When linoleum becomes spotted with paint or rust it may be cleaned by rubbing with steel shavings or emery paper.

Linseed Oil for Kitchen Floor – Boiled linseed oil applied to the kitchen floor will give a finish that is easily cleaned. It may also be painted over the draining board of the sink; this will do away with hard scrubbing. It should be renewed twice a year.

Window Cleaning Hints – The six following paragraphs will be found useful when cleaning windows:

After Polishing Windows, moisten a clean rag with a very little glycerine and rub it over the pane. Windows polished in this way do not 'steam' and will stay clean much longer.

A Cold-Weather Cleaner for Windows – Dampen a cheesecloth with kerosene and you can clean your windows quickly in cold weather when water can not be applied to the glass without freezing.

Window Cleaning Help – Before starting to clean windows carefully brush all dust off the frames. Add a few drops of kerosene to the water used for cleaning and it will give the glass a much brighter and more crystal-like appearance.

To Clean Windows – First wash the glass with water to which a little ammonia has been added and then polish with a chamois which has been dipped in water and wrung as dry as possible.

Cloths for Cleaning Windows Without Use of Water can be made with a semi-liquid paste of benzine and calcined magnesia. The cloth, which should be coarse linen or something free from lint, is dipped into this mixture and hung in the air until the spirits have evaporated and it is free from odour. This cloth may be used again and again and is a great convenience. When soiled, wash it and redip.

To Remove Paint from Window Panes – Paint can be removed from window panes by applying a strong solution of soda.

To Clean a Glass Bottle, cut a lemon in small pieces and drop them into the bottle; half-fill with water, and shake well.

Old Stocking Tops for Dusters or Dustless Mop – Old stocking tops make good dusters when sewed together. They also make good polishing cloths for oiling and rubbing down floors and furniture. Several old stocking tops cut into strips and dipped in paraffin oil make a fine dustless mop for hardwood floors.

Cheap Stain for Wood Floors – Permanganate of potash will stain a wood floor. When dry polish it with some beeswax and turpentine. It will look as though it had been that colour for years. Put the permanganate of potash in an old tin and pour about one quart of boiling water over it; then, with a brush, paint over the floor, after it has cooled. When thoroughly dry, polish. The floor will look like oak.

Cheap Polish for Varnished Floors or Linoleum – Take equal parts of kerosene, linseed oil and turpentine to make an inexpensive polish for oiled or varnished floors. An application of this polish to the kitchen linoleum with soft cloth or mop will keep it like new.

Varnish for Linoleum – To make linoleum last much longer and have a better appearance, give it a good coat of varnish every few months.

To Make Wallpaper Waterproof – To varnish the paper back of the sink, or other places, so it may be wiped with a damp cloth, coat with a mixture made with one ounce of gum arabic, three ounces of glue, and a bar of soap, dissolved in a quart of water. This amount will coat quite a wide surface.

4

IN THE SEWING ROOM

When Hands Perspire and soil the sewing material, try bathing them with strong alum water.

To Prevent Oil from Soiling Goods – To prevent a sewing machine that has been oiled from soiling the material, try the following method: tie a small piece of ribbon, or cotton string, around the needlebar near the point where it grips the needle.

When Scissors Get Blunt, sharpen them by opening and drawing backward and forward on a piece of glass. This will sharpen the bluntest of scissors.

To Tighten a Loose Sewing-Machine Belt, put a few drops of castor-oil on it; run the machine a few minutes and the belt will tighten.

To Remove Sewing-Machine Oil Spots:

(a) Wet the spots with spirits of turpentine and wash out with cold water and toilet soap, or,

(b) Rub the spot with chalk as soon as noticed.

Leave for a short time, then brush, and the spot will disappear.

To Pair Stockings – For stockings with white heels or tops, mark with indelible ink. For all-black stockings, use coloured threads, making a cross-stitch on one pair, two cross-stitches on another, etc.

To Prevent Cutting of Stockings – If the covering of the button on side elastics comes off, wind with a fine rubber band.

A Sewing Suggestion – A small, inexpensive flashlight should be kept in the sewing machine drawer. It will not only save many precious minutes, but will relieve eye strain when threading a machine needle on a dark day or at night.

5

IN THE BEDROOM

To Clean Bed Springs – To clean the dust and dirt from bed springs, set them out in the garden on a sunny day and turn the hose on them freely. The sun and wind will afterward dry them in a few minutes.

If Your Alarm Clock Rings Too Loudly, slip an elastic band around the bell to diminish the noise. The wider the band that is used, the greater will be the suppression.

Protection Against Spilled Water in Sick Bed – If water is accidentally spilled in bed when attending someone who is ill, it can be quickly dried by slipping a hot-water bag filled with very hot water between the bed covers over the wet spot and leaving it there for a few minutes.

To Clean and Polish Brass Beds – Brass bedsteads can be cleaned by rubbing them with a cloth which has been slightly moistened with sweet oil; then polished with a soft, dry duster, and lastly with a chamois leather. If this is done occasionally, it will keep them in good condition for years. But it is a better plan to use the lacquer, given below, after cleaning.

Wooden Bedsteads should be wiped every three months with a cloth moistened with turpentine to keep them clean.

To Keep Brass from Tarnishing – To keep brass beds and other forms of brass work from tarnishing, and also to avoid frequent polishing, the brass should be lacquered with gum shellac dissolved in alcohol. Apply the lacquer with a small paint brush. Clear, hard-drying varnish is also good for this purpose.

6

IN THE PARLOUR

New Way to Fasten Lace Curtains – The best way to secure lace or net curtains in place over the poles is to fasten with the very fine wire hairpins known as 'invisible' hairpins. These are so sharp that they can be pushed through the curtains without injury to the fabric, and are so fine that they are more invisible than pins. They have the added advantage of never slipping out of place like small-headed pins, or becoming entangled in the lace like safety-pins. Put them perpendicularly (up and down) in the curtain with the rounded head at the top.

Filling for Sofa Cushions – Cut a roll of cotton in small squares and put it in a pan in the oven and heat it for half an hour. Do not let the cotton scorch. Every square will swell to twice its original size and will be as light and fluffy as feathers for stuffing sofa cushions.

To Brighten Carpets – Wipe them with warm water to which has been added a few drops of ammonia.

To Clean Picture Glass – Clean the glass over pictures with a cloth wrung from hot water and dipped in alcohol. Polish them immediately, until they are dry and glossy, with a chamois or tissue paper.

Polish for Leather Upholstered Furniture – Turpentine and beeswax mixed to the consistency of thin cream makes a fine polish for leather upholstered furniture.

To Fasten Small Pieces on Furniture – For fixing on small pieces of wood chipped off furniture, use the white of an egg.

Onion Water for Gilt Frames – Flies may be kept from damaging gilt frames by going over the frames with a soft brush dipped in a pint of water in which three or four onions have been boiled. This is also good for cleaning the frames.

To Remove Fly Specks from Gilding – Old ale is a good thing with which to wash any gilding, as it acts at once on the fly dirt. Apply with a soft rag.

To Clean Gilded Picture Frames, use a weak solution of ammonia and water. Go over the gilt gently with a moist cloth, and after a few moments, when the dirt has had time to soften, repeat the operation. Do not rub hard, and dry by dabbing gently with a soft cloth.

7

IN THE BATHROOM

For Clogged Lavatory Basins – Mix a handful of soda with a handful of common salt and force it down the pipe; then rinse the pipe thoroughly with boiling water.

To Clean Bath Tub and Wash Bowl – Some house-keepers like to use kerosene in the bath tub to take off the soapsuds and stain that will gather, but the odour is sometimes objectionable. To clean the bath tub and the wash bowl in a jiffy use a half lemon rind turned wrong side out.

To Clean Mirrors – A little camphor rubbed on a mirror after the dust has been wiped off will brighten it wonderfully.

To Clean and Purify a Sponge – Rub a fresh lemon thoroughly into a soured sponge and then rinse several times. The sponge can be made as sweet as a new one.

8

IN THE LAUNDRY

To Clean Dirty Clothesline – Wrap it around the washboard and scrub it with a brush and soap suds.

Brick for Iron Stand – If a brick is used for an iron stand, the iron will hold its heat much longer than when an ordinary stand is used.

Lemon for Whitening Clothes – Put a slice of lemon, with rind on, in your boiler of clothes and it will remove stains and make your clothes white without injuring them.

To Prevent Starch from Sticking to the Iron – Borax and oily substances added to starch will increase the gloss on the article to be ironed and will also prevent the starch from sticking to the iron.

To Make Water Softer for Washing – Use four ounces of alcohol and one-half ounce of ammonia. If used for toilet purposes add to this one dram of oil of lavender. A couple of teaspoonfuls of glycerine to a small tubful of water will soften the lather in which flannel pieces are to be washed.

To Protect Hand from a Gasoline Iron – When using a gas iron, a little steam always rises from the iron and burns the hand. Before putting on your glove, rub the side of the hand well with Vaseline and this burning can be avoided.

To Prevent Woollen Blankets from Shrinking – After washing woollen blankets put them on curtain stretchers to dry and prevent shrinking.

To Restore Flannels, which have become hard and shrunken, to their former softness, soak them in gasoline.

To Make Linen Glossy – When a gloss is desired for linen goods, add a teaspoonful of salt to the starch when making.

Quick Method of Sprinkling Clothes – Turn the nozzle of the garden hose to a fine spray and sprinkle the clothes while they are on the line. All plain pieces can then be rolled up and laid in the basket as they are taken down. Starched pieces may need a little further hand sprinkling.

When Laundering Sash Curtains, never starch the hem; the rod can then be run through it without danger of tearing.

To Clean Wringer Rollers – Kerosene is excellent for cleaning the rubber rollers of a clothes wringer. After it has been applied rinse the rollers off with warm water.

When Ironing Calicoes – Dark calicoes should always be ironed on the wrong side of the goods with irons that are not too hot.

To Make White Curtains Ecru or Cream Colour – First soak curtains over night in cold water to remove all dust. In the morning wash in usual way and rinse thoroughly to remove all soap. Then put them in boiler with a tan stocking and remove when the desired colour is obtained.

To Stretch Curtains Without a Curtain Frame – Fold the lace curtain double lengthwise; then pin it on a tightly stretched line with many clothes-pins and slip a clean pole inside the folded curtain. This stretches the curtain satisfactorily and saves considerable time and money when a curtain stretcher is not available.

Right Way to Hang Skirts – In laundering skirts made of pique, cotton or woollen pin them to the line by the waistband so they will hang straight down. If pinned this way they shrink evenly all around instead of sagging, as they do when pinned at the hem.

Bleaching a Scorched Spot – If you scorch a piece of white goods while ironing, immediately rub the spot with a cloth dipped in diluted peroxide, then run the iron over it and the cloth will be as white as before.

To Iron Over Buttons, Etc. – When ironing over blouses or frocks with large buttons or hooks and eyes on, use several thicknesses of blanket or Turkish towels to iron them on. Turn the garment button-side down, and press on the wrong side. The buttons will sink into the soft padding and leave a smooth surface for the iron to run over.

To Restore Colour – When colour on a fabric has been accidentally or otherwise destroyed by acid, apply ammonia to neutralise the same, after which an application of chloroform will usually restore the original colour. The use of ammonia is common, but that of chloroform is but little known.

To Set Colour in Wash Goods before laundering. Any coloured fabric should have colour set before washing, using the method below which is best suited to the goods:

For green, blue, pink, pinkish purple, lavender and aniline reds, soak for ten minutes in alum water, using three ounces of alum to a tub of water.

For black-and-white, grey, purple, and dark blue, soak in salt water, using a teaspoonful of common salt to a quart of water; soak one hour and rinse thoroughly.

Dry in the shade. If in doubt about the goods, first try a small piece of it as above and note carefully the result.

Vinegar is also considered good for dark colours, using one-fourth cup of vinegar to one quart of water.

Sugar of lead is best for delicate greens, blues and tans. Use one teaspoonful of sugar of lead to one quart of water.

To Get Rid of Ants – To rid the house of ants, smear the cracks and corners of the infested rooms with balsam of peru.

9

MISCELLANEOUS

A Cheap Floor Wax – A satisfactory and economical floor wax which is excellent for use on hardwood floors: to one-half cake of melted paraffin add one teacupful of turpentine. Apply to the clean dry floor with a cloth; then polish with a woollen cloth or weighted brush. It gives an excellent polish and keeps the floor nice and light.

To Loosen Screws and Nails which have become rusted into wood:

(1) Drop a little paraffin on them, and after a short time they can easily be removed, or,

(2) Hold a red hot iron to the head of the screw for a short time and use the screwdriver while the screw is still hot.

To Put Hooks in Hardwood – When putting hooks in hardwood, use a clothes-pin to turn them, or slip the handle of a knife or any small steel article through the hook and turn until it is secure in the wood. This will save your fingers from aching.

Insoles from Old Felt Hats – Cut out pieces from old felt hats big enough to fit the inside of your shoes. This makes a fine insole, and is a great help to keep the feet warm.

Novelty Candle-Holders – Rosy-cheeked apples, polished and hollowed out to receive the end of a candle, make charming candle-sticks at a children's party. Especially where a colour scheme of red and white is carried out, nothing prettier or more suitable could be designed.

Lime for Damp and Musty Cellars – A few lumps of unslaked lime in the cellar will keep the air pure and sweet and also absorb the dampness.

Handy Ice Pick – If an ice pick is not available or is misplaced for the time being, an ordinary hat pin gradually forced into ice produces a crack and separates the ice without a sound. Needles and even common pins are used in hospitals to crack ice for patients.

Help in Freezing Cream Quickly – If the freezer is packed half an hour before the mixture is put in the can the freezing will be speedier. Allow three times the quantity of ice that there is of salt. Mix before using, or put in the freezer in layers.

Cutting Off Old Bottles and Their Uses – A bottle may be cut off by wrapping a cord saturated in kerosene oil around it several times at the point you wish to cut it, then setting fire to the cord, and just when it has finished burning plunge the bottle into cold water and tap the end you wish to break off. Odd shaped or prettily coloured bottles make nice vases. The top of a large bottle with a small neck makes a good funnel. Large round bottles make good jelly glasses.

Many other uses will no doubt suggest themselves to your mind.

More Serviceable Umbrella Jars – Place a large carriage sponge in the bottom of the umbrella jar to prevent umbrellas from striking the bottom of the jar and breaking it. The sponge will also absorb the water from a dripping umbrella.

Squeaking Hammock – If your hammock has an annoying squeak where the rope or chain is joined on the hook, slip the finger from an old glove over the hook before putting on the rope or chain.

To Lubricate a Clock – If your clock stops on account of being gummed with dust, place a small piece of cotton saturated with kerosene in the clock, and leave it there several hours. The fumes from the kerosene will loosen the dirt, and the clock will run again as well as ever.

A Grape-Basket for the Clothespins, with a wire hook fastened to the handle, will save much time when hanging out clothes; it can be pushed along the line and will always be handy for use.

For Worn Carpet Sweeper Pulleys – To keep the wood pulleys on carpet sweeper brushes from slipping after they have worn smooth, wrap once or twice with adhesive tape. This will also keep the pulleys from wearing unevenly with the grain of the wood.

To Protect Clothing Spread on the Grass for Bleaching – When linen pieces or small articles of clothing are placed upon the grass to whiten, much trouble may be prevented by spreading a strip of cheesecloth over them and fastening it down with wooden pegs or hairpins. This does not prevent bleaching, but keeps off worms and bugs, and prevents the articles from being blown away by the wind.

To Soften Paint Brushes that have been used for varnishing and not been cleaned, soak them in turpentine. To soften brushes that have dried paint in them soak in hot vinegar or in turpentine or gasoline.

Vinegar for Dried Mucilage – When mucilage has dried at the bottom of the bottle, pour a spoonful or two of vinegar in it, and let it stand awhile. The mucilage will be as good as ever.

To Remove Paper Labels, wet the face of the label with water and hold it near a flame or stove.

To Separate Postage Stamps – When postage stamps stick together do not soak them. Instead, lay a thin paper over them, and run a hot iron over the paper. They will come apart easily and the mucilage on the back of the stamps can be used as though it was new.

Soap Application When Eyeglasses Steam – To prevent annoyance caused by a deposit of moisture upon eyeglasses, when going from a cold into a warm atmosphere, moisten the tips of the fingers and rub them over a cake of soap. Then rub them over the lens, and polish as usual. One application every day or two is all that is necessary.

For the Invalid's Room – A few drops of oil of lavender in boiling water is excellent for the invalid's room.

For Perspiration Odour – The unpleasant odour of perspiration often causes much annoyance. Instead of using perfumery, wash the body with warm water to which has been added two tablespoonfuls of compound spirits of ammonia. This will leave the skin sweet, clean, and fresh.

For a Sprain – Salt and vinegar, bound on a sprain, will relieve the pain in a very little while.

To Prevent a Blister on the Heel – If shoes slip and cause blisters on the heels, rub paraffin on the stocking. In a short time the slipping will stop.

For Burns, Etc. – If you burn your finger or hand make a strong solution of bluing water and soak the affected part in it for ten minutes, or longer if necessary. The pain will quickly disappear and no soreness will result.

For Insomnia – A heaping bowl of bread and milk, seasoned with salt, and eaten just before retiring, is recommended as a sure cure for the worst case of insomnia.

Sulphur to Rid House of Rats – Sulphur will successfully rid the house of rats if sprinkled in bureau drawers, closets, and around holes where they are liable to come in. The farmer, also, will find that his corn will not be troubled if he sprinkles it about the barn.

To Get Rid of Mice – Mice do not like the smell of peppermint, and a little oil of peppermint placed about their haunts will soon force them to look for other quarters. Lumps of camphor placed about their haunts is another effective method of keeping mice away.

To Kill Weeds – If annoyed with dock, dandelion, or other weeds, fill an oil-can with kerosene. With a knife cut the weed off at the ground, or just below, and put a drop or two of kerosene on the heart of the weed. It will not grow again afterward.

To Take Mildew Out of Leather – Mildew on leather may be removed with pure Vaseline. Rub a little of this into the leather until quite absorbed, and then polish carefully with a clean chamois leather.

To Destroy Earthworms – To rid the earth in flower-pots of worms, mix a small quantity of finely-pulverised tobacco with the earth in each.

To Induce a Canary to Take a Bath, sprinkle a few seeds on the water. This added attraction will make the bath become a habit with the little pet.

A Cure for Leaky Pens – Empty the fountain pen and clean it thoroughly; fill with ink and apply some soap to the threads of the screw.

If Your Fingers Become Stained with Ink, wet the head of a match and rub it on the spots. Then rinse the fingers with soap and water and the ink will quickly disappear.

A Handy Pen or Brush Holder for Your Desk – A sheet of corrugated paper is a handy thing to have on your writing desk to hold wet pens or brushes. The paper will absorb the liquid and the corrugations will hold the pens or brushes in convenient position.

A Novel Match Scratcher – To avoid matches being scratched on the wall-paper almost as much as on the match-scratch, try the idea of removing the glass from a small oval or square picture frame and framing a piece of sandpaper just as one would a picture. Put a small screw-eye on top of the frame, thus allowing it to hang perfectly flat against the wall. The frame prevents the match from being carried over the edges of the sandpaper onto the wall.

Emergency White Glove Repair – If your white glove rips or tears accidentally just as you are putting it on to go out, and there is no time to mend, put a small strip of white adhesive plaster over the spot and it will never be noticed.

To Keep Rugs from Slipping – Cut a three-cornered piece of rubber sheeting to fit each corner and sew it firmly in place. Another way is to take a piece of heavy, rough sheathing paper a bit smaller than the rug and lay the rug on that.

For Sagging Chair Seats – When cane-seated chairs sag they can be tightened by washing the bottom of the cane in hot water and soap; then rinse in clean water and dry out-of-doors.

Two Uses for Velveteen – Old velveteen, fastened over a firm broom, is excellent for wiping down walls. To polish furniture, use a piece of velveteen instead of chamois leather. The former is much cheaper than the chamois and serves just as well.

Saltpetre for Icy Steps – Ice on marble or stone steps can be thawed by sprinkling several handfuls of salt-petre on it.

An Easy Fly Exterminator – To drive out flies put twenty drops of oil of lavender in a saucer and dilute it slightly with hot water. The sweet, heavy odour of the lavender is very disagreeable to the flies, and the house will soon be rid of them.

To Avoid Mistakes with Poison – When poison is kept in the house, push two stout, sharp-pointed pins through the corks crosswise. The pricking points remind even the most careless person of danger.

To Pick Up Broken Glass – Even the smallest pieces of broken glass can be easily picked up by using a bit of wet absorbent cotton, which can afterward be destroyed by burning.

For Leaky Vases or Other Ornamental Bric-a-Brac – If a valuable flower vase leaks, take some melted paraffin, such as is used over jelly-jars, and pour it into the vase and let it harden over the spot where the leak occurs. It will not leak again.

Polish for Floors – Rub polished floors with a mixture of one-third raw linseed oil and two-thirds paraffin. Afterward polish with a dry cloth.

To Prevent a Rocking Chair from Creeping across the room while rocking in it, glue strips of velvet on bottom of chair rockers, and the annoyance will cease.

To Mark Place for Picture-Nail – When just the right position has been found to hang the picture, moisten your finger and press it against the place where the nail should go. This does away with the awkward reaching for hammer and nail while holding the picture against the wall.

An Unbreakable Bead Chain – A violin string makes an excellent chain for stringing beads. It will stand a great amount of wear and tear and will practically last forever.

When Packing Flowers for Transportation – When flowers are to be sent some distance it is a good plan to place the ends of the stems in a raw potato. They will keep as fresh as if in water.

(1) *To Keep Flowers Fresh* – To keep flowers fresh put a small piece of sugar in the water.

(2) *To Keep Flowers Fresh*, place a pinch of bicarbonate of soda in the water before putting them into a vase.

(3) Cut flowers with woody stems will last much longer in water if the stalks are scraped for about three inches up.

When Taking Down Pictures in House-Cleaning Time a stick with a deep notch in the end, to lift picture-cords from hooks, is a great convenience.

To Tighten Your Eyeglasses – If the tiny screws in your eyeglasses need tightening, you will find that a small steel pen answers as well as a screwdriver.

To Mend Celluloid – Moisten the broken edges with glacial acetic acid and hold them together until the acid dries.

To Clean White Enamelled Furniture – First remove all dirty marks with a flannel cloth dipped in wood alcohol. Then wash at once with tepid water to which has been added a little fine oatmeal. Never use soap or soda.

Felt for Dining-Chair Legs – Thin strips of felt glued to the bottom of dining-chair legs will deaden the noise and save the hardwood floors.

When Baby Chokes – A choking infant can be quickly relieved by pressing between its eyes with your thumb and finger.

To Remove a Fishbone from the Throat – Cut a lemon in two and suck the juice slowly. This will soften the fishbone and give instant relief.

New Uses for Macaroni – A stick of macaroni will serve in place of a glass tube for a patient who cannot sit up in bed to drink, or will sometimes induce a child to drink its milk when otherwise it would not.

For the Restless Baby – When the creeping baby is placed on the bed for his daily nap, use a large safety-pin to pin his clothes to the bed, or to a strap fastened to the head or foot of the bed.

To Drive Nails in Plaster without cracking the plaster, put the nail in hot water for a few minutes and it can then be driven in securely without damage to the wall.

Plaster of Paris for Mending Walls – When painting walls and the plaster is in need of mending, fix it with plaster of paris mixed with some of the paint you intend using to paint it with. This will prevent the mended spot from showing. To fix a white wall, mix plaster of paris with turpentine and oil.

To Remove Smoke Marks from the Ceiling, frequently due to a smoky lamp, mix a thick paste of starch and water, and with a clean flannel cloth spread it over the entire mark. Allow it to stay on until thoroughly dry, then brush off with a soft brush, and the discolouration will disappear like magic.

To Clean a Raincoat – Use either of the two following methods:

(1) Use soap and water and not gasoline, as gasoline will injure the rubber. Lay out on a flat surface and scrub lightly with soap and water; then rinse with clear water. Do not wring. Put on a coat-hanger and hang out to dry.

(2) Pour some vinegar into a dish and dip a soft rag or sponge into it; then place the macintosh on the table and rub the soiled parts lightly.

If a Bug or Other Small Insect Gets in the Ear and causes severe pain, pour a little melted butter in the ear and there will be instant relief.

To Remove Soot from Carpet – Do not attempt to sweep the carpet until it has been covered with dry salt. Then sweep it and no smear will be left.

To Brighten a Carpet – First sweep the carpet clean. Then dip a soft, clean mop into a pail containing one-half gallon of water and one-half teacupful of ammonia; wring it well and rub it over the carpet; it will be as bright and fluffy as when new.

To Destroy Moths in Carpets, wring a thick towel out of water, spread it on the carpet, and iron over it with a very hot iron. The heat and steam will go through the carpet, thus destroying the grubs.

A Moth Preventive – If you wish to be rid of moths, pour a little turpentine in the corners of the wardrobe, chiffonier, or trunk.

To Keep Moths Out of Pianos – Try rubbing turpentine occasionally over the woodwork on the inside of the piano, and you will never be troubled with moths getting into the piano, even when it is not used for a long time.

To Clean Gilt Frames, dip a soft cloth in the white of egg and gently rub off the soiled spots.

To Remove Ink Stains from an Oak Table, lay spirits of wine on the marks; let it remain for some time, then rub well and clean off.

To Clean Leather Furniture, add a little vinegar to warm water (not hot) and brush the leather over with it. Restore the polish by rubbing with two tablespoonfuls of turpentine mixed with the whites of two eggs.

To Clean Bronze, make the article very hot by placing it in boiling water; then rub it well with a piece of flannel cloth dipped in soapsuds, and dry with a chamois leather.

To Clean Zinc – Take a thick slice of lemon and rub it over the stained spots. Let it remain for an hour, then wash the zinc metal with soap and water and it will become clean and bright.

To Clean Brass – To keep the polish on brass, after polishing in the usual way, coat with clear varnish. The following is a good polish:

To clean tarnished brass use equal parts of vinegar and salt. Rub with this mixture thoroughly, letting it dry on; then wash off in warm, soapy water and polish with a soft cloth.

Cleaning with Gasoline – The three following suggestions are made with reference to cleaning with gasoline:

(1) To take the odour of gasoline out of freshly cleaned garments, use oil of sassafras in the gasoline to the proportion of about five drops to a quart of gasoline.

(2) If a little salt is added to gasoline which is used for cleaning wool or silk material, there will be no ring remaining when dry.

(3) Put about one-third part of vinegar in the water with which you dampen the cloth when pressing an article that has been cleaned with gasoline. This will not only remove the scent of the gasoline but will prevent circles forming.

Alcohol for Cleaning White Kid Articles – Pure alcohol is better than gasoline for cleaning white kid gloves or other white kid articles, as it dries quickly without the unpleasant odour that gasoline leaves. Alcohol cleans a pair of gloves beautifully.

To Clean White Kid Shoes – Make a lather of pure white soap and milk for cleaning white kid shoes. Brush as much dirt as possible off the shoes before scrubbing with the lather.

If New Boots or Shoes Will Not Polish, rub them over with half a lemon and leave until thoroughly dry. Repeat this once or twice if necessary.

New Tag for Shoe Lace – If a tag comes off a boot or shoe lace, press a little melted black sealing wax round the end of the lace and shape it to form a tag. It will serve almost as well as the original.

To Renovate a Shabby Serge Skirt, sponge it over with hot vinegar until the stains and grease marks disappear; then thoroughly press on the wrong side with a fairly hot iron.

To Remove Shine from Woollen Goods – Wet a piece of crinoline and lay it over the shiny surface of the goods. Cover with a dry cloth and press with a hot iron. Pull the crinoline away quickly, as you would a plaster, and this will raise the nap of the goods.

To Remove Shine from Black Cloth, rub it well with a piece of flannel dipped in spirits of turpentine and dry in the open air.

To Clean a Black Dress – Take a dozen ivy leaves and steep them in boiling water. Let it stand until cold; then rub well over the stained parts. This solution will remove all stains and make the cloth look fresh.

To Clean Men's Clothing – Take a soft cloth, dip it in alcohol, and press it lightly over a cake of pure soap; then apply it briskly to the article to be cleaned. After sponging the garment carefully, press it. In cases of obstinate grease spots, rub well with a lather made from pure white soap and lukewarm water; then sponge off with alcohol and proceed as above.

Wall Paper Remover – To remove wall paper in about one-half the usual time, take one heaping tablespoonful of saltpetre to a gallon of hot water, and apply it to the paper freely with a brush. A whitewash brush is best for the purpose, as it covers a broader space than other brushes. Keep the water hot, and after a few applications the paper can be easily pulled from the wall.

To Clean Wallpaper, make a paste of three cupfuls of flour, three tablespoonfuls of ammonia and one and one-half cupfuls of water. Roll it into balls and rub it over the paper. It will make it as clean as when new.

Tobacco for Plant Insects – One tablespoonful of smoking tobacco soaked in a quart of water for twelve hours or more makes a solution that will destroy insects and promote the growth of the plant. It must be poured on the soil about every two months.

When a Wax Candle is Too Large for the holder the end should be held in hot water until it is soft. It can then be pressed into shape to fit the hole and there will be no waste of wax, as when slices are shaved off the end of a candle.

Salt Water to Clean Matting – A cloth dampened in salt water is the best thing for cleaning matting.

To Lay New Matting – Cut each width six inches longer than necessary. Then unravel the ends and tie the cords together. When the matting is taken up to be cleaned it cannot unravel and there will be no waste.

To Clean White Furniture or Woodwork – Use clean turpentine and a soft cloth to clean white enamelled woodwork or furniture. It will remove all spots without removing any of the gloss, as soap is liable to do.

To Remove Spots from Varnished Wood – Spots made by water on varnished tables or other furniture may be removed by rubbing them with a cloth wet with camphor.

To Clean Greasy Woodwork – Paint or woodwork that has become greasy can be cleaned with a cloth dipped in turpentine. Then wipe with a cloth dipped in water to which a little kerosene has been added.

To Clean Soiled Marble – Pound two parts of common washing soda, one part each of pumice stone and finely powdered chalk, mix together, sift them through cheesecloth, and make into a paste with water. Apply thickly and let it dry on; then wash well with soap and water and rub well with a soft cloth. Never use acids on marble as they destroy the gloss.

To Clean Oil Spots from Marble, first wash the stone thoroughly; then place a sheet of blotting paper over the spots and set a hot iron on it; this will draw the oil out and the blotting paper will absorb it.

Handy Fruit Picker for Farmers and Suburbanites – Take a large tomato can or other tin can and cut a V-shaped hole in one side at the top, about 1-½ inches wide and 2-½ inches deep. On the opposite side of the V-shaped hole, nail the can to a long pole. This device is useful for picking apples and many varieties of fruit from upper branches where it is almost impossible to reach them by ladder. It also prevents damage to the fruit by falling.

10

To Remove Stains Etc.

All spots and stains can be removed much more easily before washing. Fruit stains are probably the most common and they will usually disappear if the stained portion is held taut over a basin and hot water poured over and through it.

Butter or Salt for Stains – To remove fruit, tea or coffee stains from cotton or linen goods, rub butter on the stains and then wash with hot water and soap. Remove wine stains by sprinkling salt on them and then pouring boiling water through them.

To Remove Indelible Ink – Use equal parts of turpentine and ammonia to remove indelible ink when all other methods fail. Saturate the garment well, and let it soak; then rinse it thoroughly in warm water.

To Remove Grease Stains from White Woollens, use cream of tartar and water or alcohol.

To Remove Perspiration Stains – The stains caused by perspiration can be removed from garments by the application of a mixture consisting of three parts of alcohol, three parts of ether and one of ammonia.

Salt to Remove Perspiration Stains – To remove perspiration stains from clothing, soak the garments in strong salt water before laundering them.

To Remove the Stain of Mud from clothing, rub well with a raw potato.

To Remove Fruit Stains from Linen the following suggestions are given:

(1) *Fruit Stains on Linen* should be smeared with glycerine and left for about an hour; then wash the stains in warm soapy water. Repeat the process if necessary.

(2) *To Remove Fruit Stains from Linen* – Before sending table linen and white garments to the laundry all fruit stains should be well dampened with alcohol. All traces of discoloration from the fruit will have vanished when returned from the laundry.

(3) *To Remove Fruit Stains from the Tablecloth*, apply powdered starch while fresh.

Starch for Removing Blood-Stains – To remove blood-stains from material which can not be washed, cover the stain with lump starch that has been dampened to about the consistency of very thick paste. As the starch dries, the stain will go.

To Remove Mildew – The four following methods are given for removing mildew:

(1) *Buttermilk for Mildew* – Articles that have become mildewed should be boiled in buttermilk. Rinse well in warm water after boiling and hang in the sun. The same process will effectively bleach materials that have grown yellow from lack of use.

(2) *Salt for Mildew* – Mildew can be taken out by rubbing the stains well with a fresh tomato and covering with salt; afterward place garment in sun.

(3) *To Take Out Mildew*, mix equal parts of powdered borax and starch with half as much salt; moisten the whole with lemon juice, spread the mixture on the mildewed spot and place the garment in the sun on the grass. Renew the mixture every morning until the stain disappears.

(4) *Alcohol for Mildew* – Mildew may generally be removed by dipping articles into alcohol.

To Remove Road Oil – Kerosene is best to take out road oil on most fabrics, as it evaporates and does not injure same.

To Remove Wax Stains – To remove wax or tallow stains, lay a piece of brown paper over them and apply a hot flatiron. After one or two applications the paper will absorb all of the wax or tallow from the cloth, leaving no trace behind.

To Remove Tar Spots, put a little lard on the spots and let them stand for a few hours, then wash with soap and water.

To Remove Iodine Stains, immediately immerse the stained article in a gallon of water to which has been added about two teaspoonfuls of plain household ammonia.

To Remove Blueberry Stains – Blueberry stains may be removed by washing at once with cold water and white soap.

To Remove Grease Spots – To remove automobile grease, or any dark, heavy grease, from washable fabric, apply a small piece of butter and rub it in well; then wash with soap and rinse.

To Remove Tea and Coffee Stains from any white goods, soak the spots with glycerine and let them stand for several hours untouched. Afterward wash with soap and water.

To Remove Grease Spots from Tablecloths, coats, trousers, etc., sandwich the article between two pieces of blotting paper and rest a hot iron over the damaged part for a few minutes.

To Remove Rust Stains, the three following suggestions are given:

(1) *Tomato Juice for Iron Rust* – Tomato juice will remove iron rust and fruit stains from wash goods.

(2) *Rhubarb Juice for Rust Stains* – The worst rust stains can be removed without injury to the fabric by the application of boiling rhubarb juice.

(3) *To Remove Rust Stains* – Spread the rust-stained part over a bowl of boiling water and rub it with salt wet with lemon juice; then place it in the sun. Repeat this process until the stain is light yellow; then wash the cloth in weak ammonia water and afterward in clear water.

To Remove Ink Stains – The following various methods are recommended for removing ink stains:

Chinese Plan for Removing Ink Stains from Clothing – Wash the article with boiled rice; rub the rice on the stain as you would soap, and wash with clear water. If first application is not effective, repeat the process. This has been found to work like magic, even with stains not discovered until entirely dry.

A Sure Cure for Ink Stains – To remove ink stains from wash materials pour a tablespoonful of kerosene on them and rub well; then rinse in kerosene and the spots will immediately disappear. This should be done before being washed.

To Remove Ink Stains – To remove ink stains without damage to the fabric, place the stained portion over a saucer and cover the stain with powdered borax; then pour peroxide of hydrogen over the borax. Do not pour water over the borax. The stain will disappear almost immediately.

Ink Stains Can be Removed without injury to the most delicately-coloured material. Mix some mustard to a thick paste and spread it over the stain. After twenty-four hours sponge thoroughly with cold water; no trace of the ink will remain.

To Remove Ink from Linen After it Has Dried In – Wash out as much of the ink as possible in a pan of milk. Then put the article to soak in another pan of milk, letting it stand until the milk turns to clabber. Then wash out and not a trace of ink will remain.

Ink on Carpet – If ink is spilled on the carpet, wash it out at once with sweet milk and sprinkle it with white cornmeal. Let it remain over night. The next morning sweep it up and the colours will remain bright.

To Remove Ink from a Carpet, soak up as much of it as possible with blotting paper. Then saturate the spot with plenty of milk, and after some time, having removed the milk with blotting paper, rub the carpet with a clean cloth.